Finding Your Way To Your Authentic Career

ADAM TAGGART

ISBN-10: 1484826051
ISBN-13: 978-1484826058

First edition published June 2013

Dedication

To everyone wishing they weren't where they are

Table of Contents

Introduction

STAGE ONE: Taking Control of Your Professional Future
- **Step 1:** Understanding Your True Nature
- **Step 2:** Building the Life You Want
- **Step 3:** Identifying Potential Careers that Fit Both

STAGE TWO: Navigating the 'Fallow' Period
- **Step 4:** Freeing Yourself Up to Focus (Cutting the Cord)
- **Step 5:** Building Your Support System
- **Step 6:** Identifying Target Industries, Roles and Companies

STAGE THREE: Making a Successful Transition
- **Step 7:** Pursuing Work with Meaning in Your New Chosen Field
- **Step 8:** Landing the Right Opportunity For You
- **Step 9:** Beginning Your Authentic Career

Introduction

Perhaps the most frequent question asked by visitors to the Peak Prosperity website is *what should I do?* We've created a lot of content to address this broad and very far-ranging query, but at its simplest, our advice distills down to this:

1. Protect what's precious
2. Cultivate resilience
3. Live with purpose

This guide focuses on #3: finding purpose, specifically in regards to what you do for a living – your "**career**."

My work at Peak Prosperity provides me with the opportunity to speak with a large number of people each week. From these discussions, I would estimate that **over 70%** of these folks are actively dissatisfied – or, at best, unfulfilled by their current jobs.

The reasons span a wide range. Some simply experience a bad fit with the career fate steered them into; others fear their expertise will have little relevance to a future shaped by the "Three E" forces outlined in *The Crash Course*. Whatever the cause, most express a desire to switch to an entirely different profession if given the opportunity to do so.

If you're one of these folks, this guide is for you.

And its overall message is: *Your purpose is out there waiting for you.* There *is* a methodical process to find it and to transition successfully over to it.

This transition may take longer than you'd like, or at times feel more uncomfortable or circuitous than you want. But it is possible. Probable, even – if you truly commit yourself.

Introduction

For those interested in reading it, I've shared my perspective on my own journey – from dissatisfied Silicon Valley executive to rural homesteader and proud co-founder of PeakProsperity.com. A key takeaway is that I don't believe I would have successfully made the transition without either the guidance I received or the structured process I committed to.

I had tried to "figure it all out" ("find myself," "discover my calling," etc.) on my own many, many times over the past two decades – yet failing at each attempt to produce the results I wanted. I only began making true progress once I honestly admitted the following to myself:

- I did not know my own goals well enough.
- I did not have a clear methodology.
- My fears of *what if I fail?* were keeping me from considering taking truly substantive steps.

It became clear to me that to succeed, I needed to stop thrashing around on my own. It was time to bring in the professionals.

In doing so, I learned that there is indeed a process that yields the self-discovery, visioning, planning, and implementation that ultimately results in finding professional fulfillment. It has been analyzed for decades and is well-understood by competent career counselors.

There's little about this process that is novel or complex. It doesn't require you to spend a lot of money. It doesn't require you to go through any special training beforehand.

The difficulty lies in both having the courage to wrestle with yourself, as well as the reserve to see this journey through to its conclusion.

Introduction

You will be dealing with existential questions – ones that are hard for many of us to face. The answers are not likely to come easily or swiftly. You will have to get comfortable defining and categorizing yourself, which is, by its nature, also an admission of what you are "not.". Making peace with our limitations does not come easy.

Undoubtedly, there will be times when you will feel stuck, where insight and progress elude you. You will need to have the fortitude to soldier on. The process is an organic one and is therefore "messy." Embrace the uncertainty.

But if you follow this process through, the odds of you ending up with a clear understanding of your "purpose" – *and* in a job that's consistent with it – are very good.

Before we launch into the details of the process itself, know that its success depends upon:

- A Vision
- A Plan
- Permission to Change
- Perseverance

The steps in this guide are designed to help you develop these four essential success ingredients. But at the end of the day, each of these needs to come from you – and only you.

So as you begin your own journey towards purposeful work, frequently stop and ask yourself: *how well am I making progress on developing these four points?*

How to Use This Guide

Making a successful career transition takes time – typically, a lot of it.

Most of you should set the expectation that this process will take at least a year from beginning to end. For those making radical shifts in terms of industries and skills, it could take several years, depending on the entry requirements of your new field.

This is not being said as discouragement. But rather as honest truth about the scope of inner work, exploration, and perseverance a successful transition will require from you.

So, in short, approach this process as a marathon; not a sprint.

And so this guide is divided into three parts (called "stages" in this document):

STAGE ONE: Taking Control of Your Professional Future
STAGE TWO: Navigating the Fallow Period
STAGE THREE: Making a Successful Transition

Focus on one stage at a time. And don't progress to the next until you've completed the stage before.

Staying focused will help prevent you from feeling overwhelmed and becoming discouraged by the wide scope of work that successful transition requires. That's why this guide is constructed in stages.

Of course, feel free to read ahead if you're curious to learn about what the next stage of the process involves. Just don't pressure yourself to slog through the entire guide before starting Stage One.

After all, your future is waiting. So let's get started!

STAGE ONE
Taking Control of Your Professional Future
Steps 1-3

Step 1: Understanding Your True Nature

Know thyself, counseled the ancient Greek sages. The wisdom of that simple advice is just as relevant millennia later.

A better knowledge of yourself is the bedrock that you will build your future work on. This constructive introspection will be the most important work of your transition, yet it is also the area most people have invested in least thus far in their lives.

To identify a path leading to greater fulfillment, you first need to understand who you are in the *what makes me tick?* kind of way. It's from this understanding that you'll be able to unlock the really interesting and helpful insights – like *what makes me happy*? Or *what's my purpose*?

Sure – I can hear many of you thinking: *Easy for him to say. Very hard for me to do.* No doubt about it; these are very challenging questions regarding the core of your existence. Most of you have probably been asking yourself these questions all your life with less success than you've wanted.

At this point, just trust that you'll soon be able to do this much more effectively.

How?

Your first step begins with **letting go**.

If you're like most people who find themselves in an unfulfilling career, you likely feel shame or a sense of failure for ending up there. With all of the choice, opportunity, and potential that life offered to you in the past, you still managed to put yourself on a trajectory to unhappiness.

Step 1: Understanding Your True Nature

There are two really important realizations to make here:

- You are not alone.
- You have control to change your situation.

As I mentioned earlier, many – in fact, most – people are not thrilled about their jobs. Many – including doctors, lawyers, and financiers – feel trapped in their careers, stuck there due to the sunk costs of years invested, a fear of status loss, or of not being able to meet the demands of their monthly budgets (mortgage, child care, etc.).

So, right off the bat, know that you are not the only one in this situation. You have company. A lot of company.

Hopefully that helps to relieve some of the sense of failure or shame. If you've committed some social sin by not finding the perfect career yet, most of society is right there along with you.

During my own period of self-exploration, one of the most helpful insights I received was from an experienced therapist. She explained to me that part of the natural and healthy maturing process for adults is to make the transition from **living a life according to others' expectations of us** to **living one based on our own**.

For all of us, many of the decisions we made in our early lives were shaped by the feedback and expectations of others. Our parents' expectations and input were hugely influential – in most cases, playing a large determining role in what we majored in at college or which profession we chose to go into. Our friends' choices also strongly colored our early decisions. We are social creatures and are genetically and culturally wired to synchronize with those around us.

Taking Control of Your Professional Future

As we mature and develop a stronger sense of self, as well as an appreciation of our own mortality, a healthy adult begins to put aside these vestigial expectations and ask instead: *What do I want? What are my <u>own</u> expectations for myself?*

So many people are afraid of looking deep into themselves because the answers they find may be different than what others value. (My own fear was that the "best-fit" career I would discover for myself would seem "small" to others compared to the fast-track course I had been on before.)

Your key task here in Step 1 is to realize that the all of the input for STAGE ONE needs to come from within you. Society's norms and influences do not belong here.

Your goal is **authenticity**. You are seeking to develop a clearer understanding of your authentic self: the values, aptitudes, and skills that you possess. And the goals that will successfully fulfill you if attained.

This is a "garbage in → garbage out" process, which is why authenticity is so important. If you let your inputs here be colored by others' influence, you'll end up with answers that are optimized for others' needs, not yours. Focus on being brutally honest with yourself, no matter what you uncover during this introspection.

So, how to get started better understanding your authentic self?

Simply sitting down with a blank sheet of paper and trying to fit the essence of "you" onto it is really daunting. Perhaps paralyzingly so. It sure was for me.

Step 1: Understanding Your True Nature

Fortunately, I discovered three things that helped greatly in building constructive momentum. The first two are essential; the third is very helpful if you can secure it:

1. Acquire data points (the more the better).
2. Get something (anything!) on paper.
3. Recruit help.

1) Data, Data, Data
It's very hard to look at ourselves with objective eyes. But this is something you'll need to do your best at throughout this process.

The easiest way to begin to develop an objective assessment of yourself is to get data from outside sources. You'll find you can do this surprisingly quickly.

The more data you collect, the easier it becomes to get a clearer and more accurate picture on which you can then begin to base future decisions.

There are a number of readily available tests and resources that can help you accumulate useful data about your native predilections. You can also mine the perspectives of those who know you well. At this early stage, just about any data is better than none, so go forth and collect as much as you can.

Note that some of this data requires money to obtain – though not much, in the big picture, relative to the high value of finding your authentic career. In general, I think it's hard to over-invest at this stage, as the insights you gain here in STAGE ONE will yield disproportionate value as you progress through your career transition.

There are three principal types of sources that are useful here:

- Personality tests
- Aptitude tests
- Manager/peer reviews

Personality tests seek to help you understand how you prefer to exercise your perception and judgment, and will categorize you into a distinct personality "type." The rationale behind these is that by understanding your personality, you can approach your own work in a manner best suited to it.

Such tests give you a quantitative measurement on such dimensions as your level of extraversion/introversion, how you like to process information, how you prefer to make decisions, and how much structure you prefer in life.

The granddaddy of personality tests is the Myers-Briggs Type Indicator. Many of you reading this have probably taken the test at some point in your life. If you're one of those folks, see if you can dig the old results out of your attic. For those who haven't taken it or can't find their results, there are a number of options for taking the test from a licensed provider. It can also be taken online (at a cost of $39.95).

Aptitude tests strive to identify the type of work at which you are naturally gifted to succeed. The rationale (which I agree with) is that you are best served focusing your career on your natural strengths. You'll be more successful and you'll feel more fulfilled.

Several of these tests are helpful and worth your consideration:

- Gallup Strength Centers - an online service based on the Strength Finders methodology offering an introductory package for discovering your 'signature' strengths ($9.99) and a more detailed package with your complete 34-strengths profile ($89)
- CareerLeader - an online service designed to uncover your deeply embedded life interests, skills, and motivators ($95)
- Johnson O'Connor Research Foundation - an in-person, comprehensive battery of tests administered over several

days and designed to empirically determine your natural talents ($675)

I have to spend a moment here discussing the Johnson O'Connor test. Yes, this test is significantly more expensive than the others. But in my experience, it was the single most useful test I took during my transition.

In the 1920s, Johnson O'Connor was commissioned by General Electric (GE) to develop an aptitude test that could match its employees with work for which they were innately fit. Back then, an employee often spent their entire career at the company, and GE leadership hoped to get better performance if employee talent was better matched to its nature.

The tests O'Connor created worked extremely well. Later, in the 1930s, he created the precursor to the Johnson O'Connor Research Foundation (JOC), which has been administering and improving the tests ever since.

What I like about this approach is that it is extremely data-driven, and they have been iterating it for almost a century. Hundreds of thousands of subjects have gone through this process over the decades, enabling JOC to refine procedure to the point where the results are extremely predictive relative to competing methods.

The testing process consists of 6 hours of exercises designed to empirically score your natural ability across a number of specific skills. These exercises are wide-ranging; some are conceptual, some manual, some visual, some musical...some you have no clue at the time what they may be testing...

But after your 6 hours, you then have a 1.5 hour session with a specialist who synthesizes the output from your results. I found this extremely helpful, as have the people who initially put this test on my radar. While the JOC folks don't promise you'll have an 'epiphany moment', your odds are pretty good here. The goal of this exit consultation is to make sure you have a rock-solid understanding of the attributes that will most determine your career success and happiness. The researchers also do their best to help you identify potential professions or industries that are well-suited to your specific profile. So you leave the experience armed with bedrock insights about yourself, along with one or more paths to go explore.

There are JOC testing facilities in many major US cities. So if you decide you want to take the exam, you should be able to find a center within driving distance.

Management or peer reviews are also helpful vehicles for developing a better understanding of yourself. They're especially valuable sources of data if you're unable to afford any of the tests mentioned above.

If you ever worked for an organization at which you received performance reviews, now is the time to search through your files for them. As you read through these reviews, look for observations and comments that recur from year to year and/or are written by different reviewers. It's those persisting traits that are most likely to be indicative of who you truly are. When you received praise for your accomplishments, was it frequently for the same sort of skills, qualities, or domain expertise? If so, this is important data about your professional strengths.

If you don't have official performance reviews, don't worry. You can still get much of the same value (and a broader spectrum of input) by soliciting feedback from those who know you well. Set a goal to get input from 5 or more reviewers. Recruit a mix of people from your professional and personal lives.

Step 1: Understanding Your True Nature

Ask them to write down their perceptions of your strengths and your defining characteristics:

- What adjectives would they use to describe you as a person?
- What are your strengths?
- What are your "non-strengths"? (This question may be difficult to obtain answers for. Many reviewers will be reluctant to deliver criticism. Let them know you'll be happy no matter what they write here, if anything.)
- What type of work do they see you being most fulfilled by?

Again, you're looking for patterns – for observations consistent across the reviewers. If you're hearing the same things from multiple sources, it's a good indicator that the insight is likely accurate.

2) The Importance of Committing Words to Paper

Understanding who you are is a process of visualization. You want to work on building a clear and detailed image of "what is" (values, skills, goals, etc.) that you will then use as a basis for making decisions about the future.

You do this by articulating who you are. On paper.

Unfortunately, the "blank sheet" problem defeats most people before they've even begun. Why? Two main reasons:

Reason #1: A blank sheet represents unbound possibility. It's a talisman offering the promise that our lives can go in any possible direction from this moment in time. It says, *I am anything I want to be.*

Yet the very act of writing on this sheet is a *restrictive* process, because the words committed immediately stand in contrast to those that are *not* on the page. Writing forces you to choose. Suddenly limits are now being placed on your vision for yourself. This feels unpleasant – many people report emotions of anxiety and loss (the same as in the Kübler-Ross grieving process) when doing this.

Reason #2: Lack of confidence in the results. Since this is the beginning of the process, how can you be sure that what you're writing down is accurate? What if it's not, and what if the decisions you then base on these insights are horribly flawed?

Both of these challenges often present huge psychological hurdles to taking the first step towards self-visualization. Don't let them defeat you.

The trick here is not burdening yourself with "nailing" your visualization at the first try. Look at it as a process, not an event.

Just as a sculptor begins with a shapeless lump of clay, be comfortable at the beginning of the process with the fact that what you put down on paper may look nothing like anything that strikes you as the "authentic you." Like the sculptor, you will return to this work again and again, shaping here, carving there – and eventually a form you recognize will start to emerge.

The key is to just start capturing your initial thinking in written form. For those of you who are familiar with our What Should I Do? Guide, this is the Step Zero of your career transition. It's the first step that breaks the inertia and makes all of the following steps possible and easier to take.

Okay, so presuming you've now got pen and paper in hand: *What to write?*

Step 1: Understanding Your True Nature

There are four exercises that I find particularly helpful to building a clearer picture of one's authentic self:

1. Early Experiences
2. Autobiography
3. Current Life Assessment
4. The Seven Stories

I recommend that you complete each one in the order above. If you do, you will have a very solid foundation from which to build plans for your future career.

Exercise 1: Early Experiences

Your memories of your early experiences have a lot of power. This is because they occurred at a time before your personality and perspective were influenced by the more forced socialization we experience during adolescence and beyond.

As such, your childhood likes and dislikes are a good window into your core preferences. Society may shape, enhance, or repress them to varying degrees, but this core programming never really changes through life.

The goal of this exercise is to capture as many 'memorable moments' from your childhood as possible that can inform you about what your natural values and aptitudes may be.

1. Create a list (as many as you can think of) of moments in your early life when you derived pleasure from what you were doing.
   - These experiences can be from any part of your life: home, school, play, solitude. All that matters is that you have a strong positive association with them.
2. Next to each, write a brief summary of what it was about the experience that resonated for you.
3. Look through your work so far and ask, *What are the elements here that seemed to come naturally for me?* Record them.

- Was it artistic creation? Or making relationships? Or solving puzzles? Anything is fair game, as long as it felt like "fun" and not "work".

Completing this exercise should arm you with two important assets:

The first is a set of activities that feel fundamentally natural to you. You will use these later on to select work opportunities that fit your native preferences.

The second is a vestigial memory of what it feels like to be fulfilled when active. Hold on to this feeling; you will know you're getting close to the right kind of career when you find yourself experiencing it again.

Exercise 2: Autobiography
This second exercise is designed to re-introduce to you to yourself at a high level.

Write as much as you feel is needed about the following:

1. Your history
   - Focus on what is notable for you about your life so far. (What stands out as particularly good or bad?)
2. What/Who have been your biggest influences? Why?
3. What were your dreams for yourself when you where young?
4. What are your dreams for yourself now?

The objective here is to gain an understanding of the experiences and beliefs that have guided you to where you are today. Ask yourself:

- *Do my experiences suggest that I gravitate to certain types of opportunities?*

Step 1: Understanding Your True Nature

- *What are the common elements between the positive moments in my life and my dreams?*
- *How have my hopes for myself changed as I've matured?*

You want to end this exercise with a good sense of why you are who you are *right now.* Before you set your new trajectory for yourself, you need to know where you're starting from.

Exercise 3: Self-Assessment
This takes the work you started in the previous exercise and brings it down to a much more granular and tangible level.

It's designed to help you gain a good understanding of *how life is for you* right now. There undoubtedly will be elements that are just fine for you, as well as others that you wish were different.

Which is why it's very important in this exercise to be brutally honest with yourself. You are embarking on a process of change – positive change – and to do this successfully, you have to be as clear as possible in identifying the things that need to change.

This exercise is your chance to let it all hang out...to name your demons. You'll find that by putting your biggest disappointments and fears on paper, the power they have over you begins to lessen. In fact, as you progress through the remaining steps in this guide, you'll develop specific strategies and plans for moving past these regrets.

No one need ever see what you write here. So be completely open with yourself. Once you understand the full nature of the material you have to work with, you can start sculpting the vision you want.

Your Self-Assessment consists of answering the following questions:

1. What adjectives describe your life at this stage?

2. Where are you living?
3. What are you doing for work?
4. What are your relationships like with family and friends? (Be specific – list names.)
5. What interests and activities are you involved with outside of work?
6. What's the state of your physical health? Your emotional health? Your spiritual health?
7. Is there anything else particularly important to your life right now (your role in your community, etc.)?
8. What are your top priorities right now?
9. <u>KEY:</u> What are the elements you most want to change? Why?

Question #9 is especially important to flesh out. As you begin work on discovering your future career, you want to align your search parameters with work that supports these changes.

Exercise 4: Defining "Meaning" for You
This exercise, called "The Seven Stories," was developed by The Five O'Clock Club. It strives to help you put your finger on what defines fulfillment for you.

You've done a lot of living to date; this exercise leads you back through your life experiences and asks: *For you, where does meaning come from?*

As with the preceding exercises, the more time and thought you put into it, the richer the insights you will get out of it. So budget a fair number of hours for this exercise, and return to it several times over several days (at least) to review and iterate until the content feels accurately authentic.

Here are the steps to follow:

1. Create a list of 25 to 30 of the most enjoyable accomplishments you can recall from your life

- These can be from anywhere (home, work, sports, relationships, etc.). Focus on those experiences where you did something that gave you an inner sense of accomplishment.
- These need not be "big" achievements. "Small" moments (e.g., learning to bake your first pie) can be just as significant if the sense of accomplishment has the same intensity for you.

2. Pick the 7 that have the most resonance for you
3. For each of the 7, write your answers to the following questions:
   - Describe the experience (one to several paragraphs).
   - What was the main accomplishment for you?
   - What about it did you enjoy most?
   - What did you do best?
   - What was your key motivation?
   - What led up to your getting involved?
   - What was your relationship with others?
   - Describe the environment.
   - What was the subject matter?
4. Which skills you see recurring across these stories?
   - Write down the skills involved in each accomplishment. For each individual skill, add up how many times it appeared across your stories.

The key in this exercise is to look for the **commonalities** across your positive experiences. Are there themes, elements, or actions that create a common thread across each?

At end of this exercise, you should have a picture of the ingredients for meaning, as you experience it. Along with this, you should an understanding of the skills and activities you feel naturally comfortable performing.

Finishing the Exercises
With these four foundational exercises completed, you should now have a detailed and robust understanding of:

- Who you are
- How you became that way
- What you want to change
- What is important to you

These insights are critically important. They will serve as the compass points as you navigate through your journey to a new career.

3) Recruiting a Guide

The process of introspection that you're going through is challenging. It's an amorphous, non-linear process that is often emotionally taxing for a host of reasons.

Having someone (or several people) to lean on for support, encouragement, and feedback is extremely helpful for most people. As you work to build as objective a self-portrait as you can, having an outside sounding board to talk through your thinking with or receive a needed "reality check" from is very valuable.

If you can afford it, a career coach can be an excellent investment. It certainly was for me.

A good career coach is part therapist, part drill sergeant, part networking maven. The right coach will be a huge help in getting you through the testing and exercises described above (and will likely have their own preferred methods to integrate) in less time and with higher odds of success.

Step 1: Understanding Your True Nature

You want to find a practitioner who has extensive experience with career transition. Their expertise enables them to view you in relative position to the many who have gone before you. They can recognize where you are in the process, point out where you may be tripping yourself up, or identify connections you may be blind to. A good coach can literally double or triple your odds of transitioning successfully.

One note: Similar to therapists (my wife is one), career coaches have different styles. What worked well for your friend may not work best for you. I strongly advise you meet with several before deciding which one to work with.

If a career coach isn't in your budget, don't resign yourself to going it alone. You can still get a lot of benefit from a conscientious volunteer. Don't underestimate the value of a sounding board – some of my biggest epiphanies occurred as I heard myself articulate my thinking to a willing listener.

If you use a volunteer coach, find someone who knows you, but not too well. Close family members tend not to work well because it's hard for either of you to be objective – there's too much history in the way. Friends, co-workers, or fellow job-seekers are good candidates.

Whoever you end up working with, set up a regular weekly meeting to review your progress with the data collection and exercises described above. Once per week is a good cadence, as it allows you time to both execute your tasks and process them internally between meetings.

These meetings should primarily consist of you reporting your insights from the previous week. *Which specific tasks did you work on? What did you learn from them?*

Taking Control of Your Professional Future

Focus on summarizing what you took away from each task. *What did you glean about yourself? Were there any surprises? How will these insights affect your vision for yourself and your work going forward?*

Your coach is there to:

- **Add discipline** - You are going through a process. The weekly meeting is your forcing function to get your work done. If you find you are arriving to these meetings without your homework complete (or done in an overly rushed manner), it's a good sign that you're not approaching the mission with enough commitment.
- **Help you organize and articulate your thoughts** - The tasks you're working on in Step 1 produce a lot of information. These sessions force you to synthesize what's important and what you're going to do with that insight. I guarantee there will be moments when you're explaining yourself and suddenly think, *I didn't realize I knew that about myself, but it sounds spot-on!*
- **Help you see the bigger picture** - You're looking inward at this stage, and therefore can miss some of the bigger patterns and connections that an outside eye can see. This is where a professional coach can add a lot of value, especially because they are so familiar with the success factors of the transition process.
- **Provide 'tough love'** - Each of us harbors fantasies of excelling in areas that we simply aren't good at. Or perhaps we're blind to behavior traits that thwart us. A good coach will (kindly) deliver the truth when it's needed.
- **Inject inspiration** - You will inevitably encounter setbacks and low points. Having a party committed to your success who can provide encouragement and motivation is a big deterrent against burning out with your transition.

Step 1: Understanding Your True Nature

Later on, we'll go into more detail (in Steps 5 and 6) about additional ways to leverage your coach in creating a **plan** and providing **momentum**, along with the other people and resources that will round out your support team as you begin to pursue specific job positions.

But for now, invest in finding the person you want to work with.

A good source for professional coaches in your area is the alumni services center at your nearest university. Usually, there are 1-3 coaches that alumni have consistently rated higher than others over the years. Start with those.

It's becoming easier to find coaches online. The Five O'Clock Club, the Gallup Strengths Center, and CareerLeader.com will connect you with qualified coaches. Or try searching for "career coach" on Yelp for your zip code and read the reviews.

My personal preference is to work with someone located close enough to meet with in person. But I would choose a "great-fit" coach even if I had to work with them remotely (over the phone or Skype), rather than a mediocre coach in my area.

Once you've met with a few coaches and picked one, make sure that they know your goals and priorities for your career transition. Having alignment on that from Day 1 is key.

Also make sure they're aware that you're using this Guide and that they at least take the time to make themselves aware of its 9 steps. It's fine if they want to inject some changes to the plan, but only if you agree and you both make these departures a conscious choice.

Now, schedule your weekly meetings and get started! If you've already made progress on the testing and exercises before lining up your coach, that's okay. Just use your first few sessions to bring them up to speed on your work and insights to date.

Completing Step 1

If you've taken time to digest the results from the data gathering steps, and you've worked you way through written exercises 1-4, congratulations! You now have a solid sense of your **authentic self**.

You should now be able to confidently answer the following:

- *What do I value?*
- *What are my personal and professional strengths?*
- *What are my essential requirements for being fulfilled by my work?*
- *Where am I willing to make trade-offs?* (e.g., is increased happiness in my work worth a decreased salary?)

These insights will serve as the foundation stones for **Step 2 – Building the vision of the life you want**. You now know the values your future work must be aligned with, the skills and aptitudes it should leverage, and the type of fulfillment it should deliver. It should now be easier to recognize opportunities that meet these requirements (and to reject those that don't).

At this point, you should also be feeling a pride of accomplishment. You've just completed a substantial amount of the inner work "heavy lifting" that this career transition will demand.

You are now armed with self-knowledge that has powerful utility beyond your career needs. Being fully grounded in your values, the strengths you bring to the table, and your priorities will help you make better decisions in your relationships, as well as most other aspects of your life.

Step 1: Understanding Your True Nature

It will serve you well to return to the work that you've done here in Step 1 in future years. Reviewing these insights can provide valuable re-centering, if needed. Also, you can add to them as you more fully enter your new career and develop a finer sense of what "truly authentic work" means for you.

Step 2: Building the Life You Want

Now that you've waded into the waters of self-realization, it's time to dive in deep.

In Step 2, your goal is to develop your vision for the future you want for yourself. The career you pursue will need to be consistent with this vision. So it's very important to take the time you need to ensure your vision is specific, accurate and appealing to you.

There are four exercises here that will help you do this. As before, do them in order, take whatever time you need to produce them, reflect for a while, and then iterate until they feel as complete and authentic as you can make them.

Exercise 1: Future Self-Assessment
This exercise builds off of the Self-Assessment exercise in Step 1.

There, you summarized the status of your current life across a number of dimensions. Now, we're going to use that assessment as our point of embarkation on the journey to the life you want.

We're going to start by giving you permission to dream that you successfully find your way to your "authentic career," whatever it may be. Close your eyes and imagine how that would feel. Pretty good, right?

Okay, now imagine that it's 5 years from now. You've been happily engaged in your fulfilling career for a while now. *How has that impacted your life? What other changes might you have made? How would you want your life to look like at this time?*

Using the same question set as you did in Step1: Exercise 3, allow your +5 year future self to answer them:

1. What adjectives describe your life at this stage?

2. Where are you living?
3. What are you doing for work?
4. What are your relationships like with family and friends? (Be specific – list names.)
5. What interests and activities are you involved with outside of work?
6. What's the state of your physical health? Your emotional health? Your spiritual health?
7. Is there anything else particularly important to your life right now? (your role in your community, etc.)
8. What are your top priorities right now?
9. What achievements have meant the most to you?

How does your +5 year life look to you? How does it differ from your self-assessment of your current life?

Hopefully it looks like a dramatic improvement from where you are today, at least in terms of inner satisfaction. At this stage, you should feel like you're stepping into the future you were meant for – with room still left for further growth and improvement.

The exercise starts with a 5-year horizon because that's a manageable amount of time for most people. You can make some big changes in that period, but it's not very realistic to burden yourself with making a complete and total life transformation.

Now repeat the exercise, envisioning the answers you will give in 10 years' time. Pay as much attention to the elements of your life you've chosen to deepen as the ones you've worked to change. Both are helping you identify what you truly value.

If you're up for it, try answering again at +20 and +30 years. Doing so will help deepen the conclusions drawn from this exercise (though if you need to budget your time, spend the vast majority of your focus on nailing the +5 and +10 year assessments. Those are much more practical for your needs at this time.)

Be as specific as possible in painting a future that is both as optimistic yet realistic as you can hope. Because in this exercise, you are beginning to surface your understanding of **what success looks like**. We will use this as the destination for your journey (or more accurately, the idealized destination, as life is a continual journey).

Exercise 2: Writing Your Own Obituary
You probably did this next exercise in school when you were younger.

Imagine you have the chance to read your own obituary, written at the end of a long life well lived. What does it say?

Write it out. Pay attention to:

- What did you accomplish?
- What will people remember about you?
- What was most important to you about your life?
- What did your life stand for?

The goal of this exercise is to capture the essence of **who you want to be** and **what is truly important to you**. The work you choose to focus on should be supportive of both these ideals.

Exercise 3: Learnings from Past Work Experience
Make a list of the past jobs you've had. For each job, write down what you liked about it and what you didn't.

What are the answers telling you about the type of work you enjoy? What kind of culture do you seem best suited for? Did you like working in groups or on your own? Do you prefer to be a domain expert or a 'general athlete'? Do you like new challenges or prefer to hone your mastery of known tasks?

Step 2: Building the Life You Want

There are many other questions you can think of to ask yourself here. Invest the time to identify the questions that are most personally meaningful.

The objective here is to develop lists of custom requirements for:

1. What your new job absolutely **must offer**
2. What you'd **really like** your new job to offer, if possible (not essential, but what will materially make you happier in the job)
3. What your new job definitely **should NOT offer**

You will use these requirements as a filter **to intelligently identify 'good fit' employment opportunities** and to **reject those that aren't.**

Don't underestimate the power of a sound, requirements-based filter. Soon in this process, you will begin to look externally at the wide spectrum of potential job opportunities. Having a personalized filter allows to you avoid having to 'boil the ocean' and empowers you to quickly reduce your consideration set to options that truly make sense for you.

Exercise 4: Management Preferences
Similar to the past exercise, reflect on the jobs you've had in life. Think about your boss and the other managers who impacted your experience at these jobs.

Ask yourself:

*   What qualities do I want in a manager?
*   Which qualities do I refuse to tolerate?
*   What do I expect from my manager?
*   Do I want to manage others?
*   If yes, what kind of manager do I want to be? What will be my most important managerial traits to hone and develop?

Like it or not, a 'great-fit' position can be ruined by a 'poor-fit' boss. The purpose of this exercise is to arm you with a clear picture of what is desirable for you – as well as what isn't – in terms of those you work with and for.

Armed with your answered insights, it will be much easier for you now to **recognize the rare 'great-fit' job + 'great-fit' boss opportunities** when you're fortunate enough to encounter them.

Completing Step 2

This step has been about vision: enabling you to "see" the life and career you want to have.

After completing the exercises above, you should now have a clear picture of:

- What you want your life (and your work) to stand for
- Your vision for the future and how your career fits into it, with clear, specific, time-bound goals
- What elements your new career must (and must not) offer
- Your requirements in a manager

You now have a good sense of the essence of the work you want to do. From here, you will work to refine that understanding down to specific industries, companies and positions.

You now also have a clear sense of what the destination for your life looks like. You know what you are working *for*.

Moving forward with this knowledge, you are now able to **critically assess any options available to you** and ask: *Will this next step move me closer or farther from my goals?*

That's an extremely valuable ability. Your **ability to make the right decisions career-wise** has just gone up astronomically.

Step 3: Identifying Potential Careers That Fit Both

This step is about combining what you've learned in the previous two steps. You now know who you are (what you value; what your strengths are; what fulfills you) and you know what you want (your life goals; the kind of work you want to do).

What are potential career paths that offer a good fit to both?

The objective here is not to laser in to a specific position at a specific company (you'll get to this in Steps 6 and 7). Right now, you're looking simply to find the right *direction* to head in.

Get options on the table

Your job search will eventually become a process of winnowing down options in search of the 'best' opportunities. We're not there yet.

At this point, we want to get as many *viable* options on the table as possible for you to consider, investigate, and then determine what to do with.

Start by making a list of your answers to the following:

1. What jobs do I think excite me?
    a. Those you've had no prior experience with or exposure to are fair game here.
2. Who has a job that I can see myself in (eventually)? What job is that?
    a. As humans, we measure ourselves relative to others. A good way to discover an inner passion is if you reference another person and feel your gut saying, *man, I wish I could be like that!*)
    b. These can be people you know personally or simply know of (e.g., someone you read about in the news)

    c. Don't limit your options to jobs that fit your existing experience and skill set. Jobs you can see yourself becoming qualified for over time are fine candidates.
3. What industries are these jobs in?
4. What specific skills do I want to be using most in my day-to-day work?
    a. It's okay to list skills you haven't developed yet.
    b. Ask yourself, *are these skills good fits with the jobs I'm identifying?* If not, either the targeted jobs or the skills need to change.

Keeping the table clean
Your mental workspace is just as important to keep free of clutter and distractions as your physical one. If it's not, it's easy to get sidetracked.

As you work to build the list above, also ask: *What industries and jobs are BAD fits for me? Which potential options can I take off the table right now?*

Doing so is essential to keeping you headed in the right direction. Just be aware that in trying to do this, you're actually working against your genetic programming. (Thanks a lot, Mother Nature).

Evolution influenced human behavior towards a preference for keeping as many options open to us as possible at all times. That way, when unexpected danger arrives (say, a hungry saber-toothed tiger) we have the greatest odds of making it out of trouble alive.

This evolutionary predilection is actually a handicap when it comes to career searching. To optimize, you have to specialize. In other words, to find the best path, you have to close the doors to all the others.

But we don't like to limit our options because it makes us feel more vulnerable. And so, many people waste valuable focus, energy and time entertaining options that are not in their best interests. Maybe it's because society (peers, parents, the media) tells you a certain career is 'hot' right now. Or maybe because it's a "good opportunity" for the career track you're currently in.

The key question here is: Is it 'hot' or 'good' for *you*, given the success requirements you developed in Steps 1 and 2? If not, don't waste time considering it.

Exercising the muscles to say "no" to opportunity is a critical practice to master. That's why this guide starts with the exercises it does. You now have all of the insights to know if a potential job is compatible with your values and goals or not. You can now give yourself permission to turn down possibilities – no matter how popular with others. Doing so will actually relieve you of stress, as you're no longer forcing yourself to pursue leads that don't feel authentic. And you'll be giving yourself the gift of extra capacity to focus on the leads that are.

Completing Step 3
The objective of this Step is straightforward: to end with a substantial list of potential 'great-fit' industries and professions based on your newfound insights about yourself.

This list reflects **your best estimation – given what you know right now – of the territory in which your authentic career lies.**

In the next three Steps (in STAGE TWO), you will explore these opportunities in increasing detail to learn which ones are indeed great fits, and which aren't (despite their initial promise or appeal).

Completing STAGE ONE
It's very important to complete in full each of the three steps of this stage before moving on to STAGE TWO.

If you have – congratulations! You've just figured out *what* you're supposed to do with your life.

Now it's time to figure out the *how*.

In STAGE TWO, you will start mobilizing behind the very deliberate trajectory you've calculated here in STAGE ONE. Up to now, your journey has been inward-facing. Now it's time to start engaging with the outside world.

You'll focus initially on securing the resources and support you'll need to maximize the odds for success in your career transition.

Once that's done, you'll begin a very measured process of developing a target list of specific professions, positions, and businesses.

Prepare yourself. This will be the least linear and most ambiguous stage of your transition, which is why it's often referred to as "the fallow period."

Why is it called that? Because uncertainty and lack of clarity are normal here. In fact, they're necessary.

The fallow period is a time where you are synthesizing a lot of new information – which takes time for your brain to fully process. It needs time to sift through the different options you're learning about and measure them against the priorities you've set for yourself in STAGE ONE. Give yourself time to have experiences, sit with them for a while, and be ready for insight when it arrives.

Taking Control of Your Professional Future

By the end of STAGE TWO, you will have a very short list of career options that are highly likely to be 'great fits' for you. You will have heavily researched these options, and so your confidence in their likely fit will be very high. You'll have developed the relevant networks to help you locate or create a suitable entry point.

In short, you'll be prepared for making the full-court press for the best job of your life.

For Inspiration: Wendy's Story

Career changes? I've done a couple of those.

The first was in my 30s – from "whatever job I could have" to a structured career. After having to come home from college (first-year nursing) due to a family illness, I'd sort of fallen into restaurant work. But that was a J-O-B; a way of bringing in money I had no passion for.

In my case, I wanted to transition from restaurant work into safety management. The two paths available to me at the time were through safety OR management, and I chose the management path, since management skills were transferrable. So I worked my way up into restaurant management. There was a hiatus where I ran my ex-husband's construction business office from home, but I incorporated that, too. Eventually I went into construction safety management.

*My second career change started about seven years ago, when I had become a successful construction safety manager. I was 50. I saw the writing on the wall: Construction does not do well in an economic contraction, and we were in for a **mother** of a contraction. I also looked at retirement options and knew our government was broke and could not keep its promises. My new goals were to (a) move out of the unsustainable Boston-to-DC Megalopolis to an area with a lower cost of living and slower pace, and (b) find a job where I could telecommute. The two potential paths I narrowed my consideration set down to were (a) to work from a home I'd buy in the mid-west on my own OR (b) marry someone in a slightly more populous area than the mid-west. Retirees who are married live longer, so I chose that option.*

I ended up marrying a man with a paid-off home in the much-cheaper, quieter, less populous South, and I started my own safety consulting firm that allows me to work from home. I'm much more efficient doing work I love, and without a commute, I have time to learn skills like organic home vegetable gardening, canning, and seed-saving. Since my husband has a good pension plus a 401K, I took the tax hit, took the money out of my self-directed IRA, and put it into my new career, home energy efficiency, and self-sufficiency gear for us. It paid the start-up costs for my business. We got solar hot water, solar cells, an airtight wood-burning stove, solar attic fan, Eco-foil attic insulation, screen doors and windows, solar panels, a huge square-foot garden, fruit trees, canning supplies – you name it. And we have shared goals, and each other.

Why am I sharing this? Thanks to knowing what I wanted and going after it with a definite plan, I had an intentional life. My first career change took a long time (years), but that was mainly due to me needing a college degree and a professional license while raising kids, all of which took time. But I ended up where I wanted to be. The second transition took less time because the home business was based on my old career. The hardest part of that was finding a decent, like-minded spouse at my age, but I did that scientifically and wrote a book on that, too. I have time to write now. It's great.

STAGE TWO
Navigating the 'Fallow' Period
Steps 4-6

Step 4: Freeing Yourself Up to Focus (Cutting the Cord)

It's time to commit yourself fully to seeing your transition through.

In many ways, this is the toughest Step emotionally. Why? Because it requires the biggest leap of faith in the entire career transition process.

You're ready: You've done your foundational planning. You know who you need to be, you know your success requirements, and you've got informed bearings by which to navigate.

But you don't have the security of specifics yet. You haven't yet zeroed in on the exact industry or company yet. There's no guaranteed job offer in your hand.

In order to secure those specifics, you're going to have to slog through a lot of ambiguity. You're going to be gathering and assimilating a tremendous amount of information – your mind is going to need a good deal of time to process and come to conclusions.

You need to free up the capacity for that information gathering and synthesis to take place.

To be successful in this Step, you must:

- Create substantial **dedicated time** in your weekly schedule for your transition work
- **Seclude yourself** from constraints and pressures
- **Embrace the uncertainty** and ambiguity you will experience in STAGE TWO
- **Trust in yourself** to succeed

Step 4: Freeing Yourself Up to Focus

Creating Sufficient Capacity
You've likely heard that finding a new career feels like taking on an entire second job if you're already employed. That's completely true.

The hard truth is, the more time you can give your transition work, the faster and more successful the process will be.

Of course, most of us are pretty exhausted by the demands of our existing job (and life in general!). So how do you shoehorn in the career search?

There's no magic answer here. You have to do two things:

1. Prioritize your transition work over your current job
2. Make the time. Remove other commitments from your schedule and dedicate the time to your search.

You need to make peace with the fact that if you give your career search and your current job equal priority, you're going to do a substandard job on both. Would you rather underperform for a period in a job that doesn't fulfill you, or do you want to risk undermining your chance of finding work that truly fulfills you? The choice should be obvious.

If you truly want to find your authentic career, this is the time to step up and own your dedication to the process.

Yes, it's a bit scary to intentionally decide to risk underperforming at work, especially if your income may suffer. But it's a necessary risk if it frees up the time you need. It's a cost that will pale in comparison to the gains of making a successful career transition.

And speaking of time, you need to dedicate *hours* each week to your search work. Two hours per week is an absolute minimum, and that's for the folks with truly insane schedules. There really isn't a weekly maximum.

Navigating the 'Fallow' Period

In fact, it's best if you can truly 'cut the cord' from your old, 'poor-fit' career and dedicate yourself full-time to your transition. In other words, **if you can, quit your current job**.

I realize few people feel they can emotionally stomach or financially afford to do this. I thought I was one of them. But it's what career coaches recommend *if you can do it without undermining your chances for success.*

During my own transition, I ended up making such a 'clean break,' even though the thought of doing so initially petrified me.

I thought the switch to negative cash flow and the uncertainty of not knowing where the happy finish line to this process was (or even if there was going to be one) would turn me into a nervous wreck. The truth is, it did. For the first few days.

But then things changed for the better. As my career coach had predicted, leaving my 'poor-fit' path soon brought me to feel as if a tremendous weight had been lifted. I was no longer chained to a path I knew in my heart wasn't right for me. With that liberation came the freedom to focus on pathways that held the promise of being much more compatible with the foundational insights I had uncovered in STAGE ONE.

I also began to feel excited. While I was still pretty anxious about not knowing what I was going to do, I realized that the surefire way to fail was to not try. As the lottery folks say, *you can't win if you don't play.* And I was finally playing. 'Winning' was now finally an option.

(Personal aside: I have a strong antipathy for lottery systems of all types. But I do like this catchphrase.)

The other benefit that breaking from your current job offers is the discipline of working without a safety net. You definitely work harder and are more committed knowing that failure is not an acceptable option. Many accomplished entrepreneurs attribute this "all-in" approach to their success, reflecting that if the risks hadn't been so high, they likely wouldn't have pursued their dreams hard enough to achieve them.

But even if you decide you can't take the drastic step of leaving your current job, success is still entirely achievable. It will just likely take longer.

And whether or not your new career hunt is a full- or part-time endeavor, you need to treat it as the top priority it is. Keep a calendar dedicated for this process. Block off scheduled hours for your transition work each week. As mentioned earlier, 2 hours per week is the absolute minimum.

Honor that time commitment. If you find yourself bumping this work time for other commitments, it's a clear sign that you're not employing the dedication you'll need to succeed. Either re-up your commitment, or shelve your aspirations until you can.

Shielding Yourself from Limiting Factors
A positive attitude is a powerful asset in managing through the uncertainty of the Fallow Period. You'll want to create a workspace that fosters one.

For many people, that means limiting your time with the people who know the "old you," especially those who aren't aware of your transition plans or who don't appreciate them. In general, human beings don't like change. Our natural response is to resist it. Don't be surprised if folks who know you well try to talk you out of taking any "drastic" steps.

Navigating the 'Fallow' Period

This can manifest powerfully in those who are dependent on your income, notably spouses. Be aware that financial fears may cause your partner to consciously or sub-consciously discourage your quest for a new career.

Understandably, this can have a serious undermining impact to your confidence and morale.

While there are no magic solutions here, some basic recommendations are:

- Share the rationale for your transition. Let them know you're doing it, ultimately, to be a better, more complete partner.
- Assess their level of support for your decision.
- If low, only share essential updates going forward and consider couples therapy, if possible. (While it's best to have an engaged supportive partner than not, it's preferable to have some distance during this period versus battling an actively opposed partner.)

Only slightly less important to manage than your relationships is your workspace.

Find one where you can focus uninterrupted; ideally one that is **not** shared. Being able to quickly slip into "work mode," with all of your resources and records in their known places, will be of great value – especially if you only have a few hours a week available.

Embracing Uncertainty
As forewarned, STAGE TWO is characterized by ambiguity. Your journey here will be difficult at times. You'll feel anxious. You will likely often feel like you're *regressing* versus *progressing*.

That's okay. It's *supposed* to feel this way.

Step 4: Freeing Yourself Up to Focus

The human brain needs time to take in data, formulate assumptions, explore them, and then change them based on new findings. Just like navigating a maze, you sometimes need to backtrack to determine the right path forward.

The key here is to prepare yourself mentally for this. Respect the need for the "squishiness" of the process. Have confidence that as you go through it, things will eventually start resolving into a clear course of action.

If you don't, you run the risk of stalling out. If you end the process early because you're not progressing each day in a pure linear pattern (which is simply not realistic), you will soon find yourself right back in the angst of your original dilemma: stuck in a 'poor-fit' job, yearning for a better future.

Instead, as best you can, embrace the uncertainty. Remember, nothing worth having is ever achieved without risk.

Trusting in Yourself
The ambiguity of the Fallow Period is conquered by continuing to place one foot in front of the other until you reach firmer ground.

Trusting in yourself, in your ability to blaze a path to a better career, dramatically helps both your odds and your psyche during this period.

Cultivating this self-confidence will serve you well long after this transition process is over. So, exercise and develop the muscles for it now. There's really no reason not to.

Remember, you've already made it this far. You've identified the need to make a big change – for the better – in your life. You've unlocked the secrets of your authentic self and crafted the requirements of the work that will make it happy.

You've committed yourself to seeing this change through. So, why shouldn't you have confidence? You've made more progress in self-development recently than most people do in a decade (or two).

Give yourself the respect of self-respect. You'll sleep better. And perform better in this transition, too.

Completing Step 4
Step 4 is all about getting ready to dive into the pool.

The guidance provided in Step 4 is geared toward getting you emotionally and physically ready for the rigorous and challenging (but rewarding!) period of work immediately ahead of you.

If you've successfully prepared yourself, the rest of STAGE TWO should feel bracing, even fun. Because you're entering 'kid in a candy store' mode, where you're looking at a lot of appealing options and working on winnowing them down to the sweetest one for you.

In Step 5, you'll finish outfitting yourself with all of the resources you'll need in your new career hunt. And Step 6 will see you venture out into the field.

Step 5: Building Your Support System

Now it's time to put the odds as unfairly in your favor as we can.

You've committed yourself to your transition. You've taken your leap of faith into ambiguity. Now let's make sure you have gathered as many people as possible with vested interests in your success and that you have all the tools you'll need going forward.

Step 5 focuses on assembling an "unfairly good" support system. Robin Hood had his merry men. Frodo had the Fellowship. James Bond has Q. Why shouldn't you have your own squad of zealous helpers?

Specifically, you want to recruit the following people before you begin your job search in earnest:

- A career coach (professional or volunteer)
- A support group of other job-seekers (in your local area and/or online)
- Advisors (people whom you can tap for perspective)
- Networkers (people you can tap for contacts)
- Emotional supporters

Take care in assembling this team. Every member should be selected for specific reasons – they must have skills, relationships, or knowledge that will benefit you.

And you want them directly motivated for you to achieve success. Each should be clearly aware of what they will get out of helping you (e.g., money; support in return; a happier spouse). You may be leaning on them heavily at times, and you don't want them to regret or resent their participation.

Navigating the 'Fallow' Period

Your Coach (Revisited)

In Step 1, we introduced the great advantages that having a coach bestows. Hopefully, you've already benefitted from one firsthand in your progression here to Step 5.

But if you've made it this far without a coach, I strongly encourage you to consider finding one now.

Coming up next in Step 6, you'll build your action plan for zeroing in on the specific position(s) you want to apply for. After that, you'll design a plan of attack for landing them.

Having someone to serve as sounding board/planning partner/mentor/butt-kicker during this time is invaluable. In this process you'll be inundated by information, juggling a lot of tactical tasks, and feeling emotionally tapped.

Your coach is there to keep you on task, moving forward, and true to your goals. As you enter farther and farther into the trees, they help you continue to keep perspective on the forest.

Bottom line: Get someone to fill this role for you if at all possible. An experienced professional is preferred, but a willing friend is better than no coach at all.

Your Support Group

They say "misery loves company." But, it turns out, so does opportunity.

Other people in the midst of their own career transition are a fantastic (and free) source of emotional support, best practices, employer insights, and job leads.

Join up with compatibly minded job seekers in your local area to create a support group that will benefit all of you. You won't regret it.

Step 5: Building Your Support System

A well-functioning support group:

- **Exists to keep its members moving towards their goals** - This is the 'brotherhood of the foxhole.' Each of you is looking to the other to help make sure that you emerge from the experience with your goals achieved.
- **Helps you crystallize your thinking** - As you share your results each week, you explain what you learned and how your planning will change as a result.
- **Delivers insights** - Your fellow group-mates will have expertise or access to information that you don't. Tap them for insights that will benefit your strategic decision-making (e.g., industry intelligence) or tactical planning (e.g., new career listings)
- **Delivers tough love when needed** - You're not likely to bring your A-game every week to the career search. If necessary, your group-mates will deliver the honest feedback you need to hear if they believe you're shortchanging yourself.

Fill your support group with people you don't know well, if at all possible. It will help you be more honest and open about issues that you may feel uncomfortable or embarrassed sharing with those closer to you.

If you need help finding other job seekers to meet as a group in your local area, here are some resources that should be able to connect you with candidates:

- Alumni career service departments of nearby colleges
- Craigslist.com Discussion Forums (click "jobs" and let folks know where you're setting up a group)
- Your town's Chamber of Commerce

Navigating the 'Fallow' Period

Once you've recruited your first few members, pick a time and place for a regular weekly meeting. Share your goals, your transition plans as they currently exist, and your priorities for the next week. These short-term priorities are the most important, because each week you will report on your success in pursuing them and what impact the findings have had on your transition.

You may also want to find a location (e.g., a café with wi-fi) where you can gather in between group meetings to work – not to discuss, but to simply have the presence of others working alongside you to model and provide motivation .

A good way for your support group to stay in touch throughout the week, share a calendar and interesting articles, etc., is to use the online Groups at PeakProsperity.com. They're simple to create and give your real-life group an immediate platform for coordinating. There are a number of other online group platforms to consider if you want to kick additional tires (like Yahoo! Groups and Ning).

I'd recommend keeping your support group to 6 people or less in size. More than that and it becomes hard for an individual voice to get the spotlight long enough to be meaningful.

If you're having trouble finding enough people in your local area, then consider joining or creating an online support group. You lose a little of the ease and the intimacy of sitting around the table with the others, but the power of the union is still largely there. Again, the online Groups at PeakProsperity.com work well for this (start by searching the Groups for "job" or "career" to first see if there are any existing groups you'd consider joining).

Step 5: Building Your Support System

Your Advisors
Advisors are domain experts, meaning that they have deep experience or knowledge of a specific industry or skill area. Their role on your team is to offer seasoned perspective on the bigger decisions you'll face in your career search.

As you begin to identify the sort of work you want to pursue, identify 2-5 good minds that could potentially serve as advisors. Seek them out, being very respectful of their time and the fact that you will likely benefit much more from this relationship than they will.

A good advisor is someone who has already reached the peak of his or her profession and is motivated by helping 'new blood' enter it as (or avoid it, depending on fit) as gracefully as possible.

A good advisor can save you weeks or more of painful learning-curve climbing if used correctly. They are best approached with specific questions or presented with a decision you are going to make and your rationale for making it. They have likely been in your exact situation many times and have an excellent assessment of the probable outcomes.

However, avoid dumping open-ended problems in their laps (e.g., "What should I do with my life?") You'll find your time with them cut short if they feel you're asking them to do your own hard work for you.

In the same way, be careful of tapping your advisors too much. They are there to provide guidance at key decision points. Abuse your access to them, and you will likely find them absent when you need them most.

So be sure to express your gratitude sincerely and often. Sending a thank-you note following a session is a must.

Navigating the 'Fallow' Period

Your Network
Starting with Step 6, you'll be out targeting people to talk to. Lots of people.

You'll be building your own list of valued contacts in the process. But it's so much less time-intensive if you can leverage someone else's. And just because you have someone's email address doesn't mean they'll respond to you.

In his popular book, *The Tipping Point*, Malcolm Gladwell talks about the importance of "connectors." These are folks who know an abnormally large number of people and enjoy making introductions. (For those interested, Gladwell would catalogue your advisors as "mavens.")

If at all possible, you want to be on good terms with a few solid connectors.

As you start to locate industries and/or companies of interest, connectors can quickly get you an informational phone interview or an in-person audience. This is orders of magnitude faster and more successful than the "cold contact" approach.

As with your advisors, treat your connectors with kid gloves. And, when relevant, connect them with the interesting contacts you meet during your transition journey. Relationships are currency for connectors, so be sure to pay them back as you can.

Your Emotional Recharger
As mentioned, the "hunting" part of your career search is about to start in earnest.

You're going to get tired from the work. You'll experience some setbacks. Frustration at some point is a guarantee.

Step 5: Building Your Support System

To prevent burnout, you need someone, or some people, who will help you emotionally recharge. Folks you can vent to, who will help you forget the stresses of the job search for a while. Who create an environment where there's no judgment or prying, where you can just be yourself.

A supportive partner and/or a close friend often play this role best. If neither is available to you, join a league around an activity you enjoy (pick-up basketball, quilting – whatever!) and use that to blow off steam. Or your parents, a sibling, or perhaps your spiritual advisor would be willing to fill the role.

Try your best to line up someone you can count on to be there for you when/if things look dark. Make sure they're aware in advance of what you're looking for from them. And let them know you'll be there to provide similar support for them in the future whenever they may be going through a similar life stage.

Your Arsenal
In addition to these key relationships, there is a select number of tools that you must have in your career-transition tool kit. These will help you **stay organized and updated**, two essential ingredients for success:

- **Contacts book** - You will be reaching out to and hearing from many more people during this time than you are used to. The value of your email account and your phone at this time can't be overestimated. Whenever you make or learn of a contact with potential to help you, capture it! (You can periodically weed out those that don't prove useful.) BACK UP THIS INFORMATION OFTEN! Once you complete your transition into your new career, your address book of industry-specific contacts will be worth gold to you.
- **Calendar** - Your search benefits from structure. As Step 4 recommends, block out hours each week dedicated to your search. As you build momentum, you will need to schedule calls and meetings, attend conferences and

perhaps classes. You will need to block off time to prepare for these, too. Your calendar is your key to remaining dependable. Forget to put it on the calendar, and your odds of unintentionally dropping a commitment increase dramatically. That's NOT the way to impress a potential new employer.

- **Document filing system** - As unsexy as it may sound, an intuitive, well-organized filing system can make a big difference. Being able to retain and retrieve intelligence when you need it has power. And a disorganized workspace is guaranteed to result in lost data and time. Do yourself a big favor and invest early on in figuring out the process you want to use for cataloging emails and documents related to your job search (I relied heavily on dedicated folders), as well as developing a filing system for your physical paperwork.

- **Information sources** - Learning about your target career(s) and staying up-to-date are critical elements of your transition. Fortunately, the Internet makes that substantially easier these days than it used to be:

  - **Websites** - Read the websites that those in your target profession(s) read. As you learn of new ones, bookmark them.

  - **RSS readers** - Many of the websites you bookmark have RSS feeds. Consider using a popular RSS reader (e.g., My Yahoo!) to aggregate all of the headlines from these sites onto one page. This way, you don't have to visit each site individually to see what's new.

  - **Search alerts** - Instruct your favorite search engine to email or text you with alerts when industry news of interest to you is published. Set keyword alerts for the companies you look at, or key industry topics.

  - **Social media** - Use of Facebook, Twitter, LinkedIn, Meetup.com, Instagram, Pinterest, and other social media formats is exploding right now. Some of them you must use; some you should consider. You also need to be aware of pitfalls to avoid:

- LinkedIn - This site pretty much falls in the 'must use' category for those considering a standard, corporate job. The role of the paper-based resume has been replaced by your digital LinkedIn profile, which is akin to a resume on steroids. Just about all recruiters these days start by looking at a candidate's LinkedIn account.
- Facebook - *Dos:* If the companies you are looking at have a Facebook page, you should "like" them and keep tabs on any updates they post. *Don'ts*: You must assume that your potential future bosses will check out your Facebook page. Don't have any comments/pictures/etc. there that you would be embarrassed for them to find.
- Twitter - Similar to an RSS reader, Twitter can be an excellent source of industry insider insight. Find the opinion leaders in the industries that interest you and "follow" them. Since you likely have more time to spend on Twitter than the people who will be interviewing you, you'll soon find that you may be more up to speed on breaking industry trends than they are.
- Meetup.com - Meetup.com often holds "meetups" in the physical world for people of similar interests and professions. Search the site for any relevant events near you.
  - **Trade publications** - Most industries have trade publications that are highly influential (such as *The Wall Street Journal* and *The Economist* for the finance industry). Learn which are relevant to your career search and start reading them. Most of these are now online, so add them to your RSS reader.

- ○ **Canonical books** - Similar to the trade publications, there are usually seminal books that had great impact on the industry (again using finance as an example, think Benjamin Graham's *The Intelligent Investor*). Have your advisors draft up a shortlist of the most important books for you to read (or skim, at least).

- **Resume and References -** Your first impression with most people will happen digitally. So invest the time to present well.
  - ○ **Resume** - Your resume is still the main vehicle someone who doesn't know you uses to get an initial sense of who you are. Therefore, create one and take it seriously. Realize that most reviewers look at your education and your most recent experience, and little else. The former is what it is, but make an effort to have the latter appear as relevant to your target career as possible.
    - ▪ As mentioned above, your LinkedIn profile will be used much more than your resume. But if you write your resume first, creating your LinkedIn profile will be a snap.
  - ○ **References** - Line up your references early, and ask them for a written reference (no more than several paragraphs) with permission for you to share with prospective employers. They should focus on how your prior experience qualifies you for the career you're targeting. (If it doesn't, have them focus on the relevant aptitudes and skills)

Completing Step 5
If you have lined up the resources above, you are now **fully outfitted for your transition.** *You're ready.*

You're now prepared for the "wet work": networking, informational interviewing, and research, research, research. Things are about to get busy. You're through with *preparing* and about to start in with the *doing.*

But with so much now in your favor, with all of the methodical preparation you've done, you should hopefully feel excited and exhilarated.

You are now stepping into the world that best suits you. Every step from now will be bringing you closer to your authentic career.

Step 6: Identifying Target Industries, Roles and Companies

Time to roll up your sleeves and dig into the dirty work.

In Step 6, you will validate your earlier estimates of 'great-fit' industries and jobs. In doing so, you will winnow down the set of available options until you have the visibility and confidence to start making firm decisions.

You know how people will sometimes refer to their profession as their "chosen field"? Well, your goal by the end of this Step is to choose a field – the *right* field.

Hopefully that sounds exciting to you. It should. In fact, it should be inspiring: The long stretch of asking *what should I do?* is about to conclude with a good answer. In fact, the *best* answer you could have hoped for. Because it will be custom-tailored to you, based on all of the work you've done leading up to this stage.

But this may also sound a bit intimidating. It sure sounds like it's going to require an awful lot of work.

That's right. It will.

But the good news is, you're prepared for it. And it's not rocket science. If you apply yourself, commit to the hours, and keep your end goal in mind, your chance for success here is almost a guarantee.

You just have to have the fortitude to see the process through. And if you've completed all of the Steps prior to this one, the odds that you have the required perseverance are quite high.

So enough talk. Let's get started!

Step 6: Identifying Target Industries, Roles & Co's

Research, Research, Research
Review the list of potential 'great-fit' jobs that you created in Step 3.

In that exercise, your objective was to get as many relevant options onto the list. In Step 6, the objective is to remove as many options as possible, leaving only the ones most compatible with your requirements.

Before you can start removing options, you need to learn all you can about each of them. As you take in new information about a certain job, ask yourself: *Does this new insight make the opportunity a better or worse fit for me?* If the answer is "worse," then ask: *Is it so much worse that this job is no longer a "great-fit" candidate?* If the answer to that question ever becomes "yes," strike it from the list.

So, how to best research these jobs? Simple: Put in the hours with the resources you've already put in place.

In Step 5, you assembled a portfolio of support resources. Now is the time to start using it.

Read as much as possible about the industries and jobs you identified in Step 3. Plow through the websites, headlines, news alerts, and social media feeds that you previously set up. Have time dedicated for this daily, if possible. Spend your evenings with the trade publications and canonical books. After a few weeks, you should have your finger solidly on the pulse of the industries you've identified. After a month or two, you'll have as much "book knowledge" about the field as just about anyone.

As helpful as this knowledge is, it's all academic. It doesn't give you a good sense of the day-to-day tasks or the level of fulfillment you may experience if embedded in the work. You'll need to supplement this learning by talking with people who actually do this for a living. We'll talk more about that in a moment.

63

However, if you find yourself disinterested by what you're learning, or realizing that your earlier, less-informed understanding of a particular profession was romantic but wrong, you may be able to use this insight to strike options from your "great-fit" list early in the process.

Network, network, network
Once you've got some solid reading time logged (at least 2 weeks) and you know just enough to be dangerous, it's time to start networking.

You want to talk with 2 types of people:

1. Those who can clarify your understanding
2. Those who can help you get the job you want

It's not uncommon for one person to fall into both camps, but at this earlier stage, you want to focus more on talking with the first type of folks.

This is all about **networking**. You want to talk with veterans who have actual expertise in the careers you're considering. And you want to talk with a *lot* of people.

You want as much data and as many perspectives as you can get. Why? Because people are different. You're invariably going to get a range of answers and advice in these discussions. Take the things you hear repeated most frequently as fairly rock-solid facts about the career. Take the rest in the context of the source. If you've received lots of differing feedback, ask yourself: *Which came from sources most like me?* Those are your best proxies for how you will likely perceive reality if in their job.

Step 6: Identifying Target Industries, Roles & Co's

Create a list of the specific people you want to talk with. If you don't yet know who they should be, prioritize the list of industries, companies, and/or professions you most want to learn about. Then look for people who work in them. Update this list each week as your targeting becomes more informed and refined.

You've heard of the '6 degrees of separation'? The good news is, it's now actually more like 2 to 3 degrees. Meaning that if there's somebody you want to talk to, chances are you know someone who can directly connect you to them, or you know somebody who knows somebody who can.

Bring your list of targets to the networkers you identified in Step 5. Ask them to make introductions for you to the folks they know. If they don't know one of your targets personally, chances are good that they know someone who works in a similar position who will be a good substitute.

In addition to your networkers, explore your college's alumni network (most are online now) as well as LinkedIn. Both make it very easy to locate professionals by industry, company, and title. Alumni are usually happy to take time to talk with you. LinkedIn 'cold contacts' (via InMail) are much more hit-or-miss, but definitely worth the outreach.

Also, be sure to talk to people at all levels within the industries you're researching. Not only will you get different perspectives and a well-rounded sense for what success requirements at different levels are like, but you will also reduce the odds of bad information. Sometimes people are reluctant to open up to outsiders because they fear you could replace them. This concern is less of an issue among people higher or lower within the organization.

Navigating the 'Fallow' Period

When making first contact with a target, email is the best medium to use in most cases. Keep it short. Let them know this is informational only – you aren't asking them for any favors or commitments. Give them a concise sense of what you want to talk about and why they are the right person for you to be talking to. Give them an extremely brief sense of who you are, but DO NOT send along your resume at this time. Resumes are work to read; no one enjoys it. You don't want to start your relationship by putting a burden on your prospect.

An example of a fine outreach email reads like this:

To: Joe Target
CC: John Referrer

Subject line: Referral from John Referrer

Body:
Mr. Target –

In a recent conversation I had with John Referrer, he recommended I reach out to you.

After 15 years in IT, I'm in the process of transitioning to a career in the alternative energy space. I'm specifically interested in learning more about the future of passive solar solutions. Given your corporate development role at PassiveSolarXYZ Inc., John thought you would be an excellent source of insight for me.

Would you be open to answering a few questions over the phone?

If so, please let me know a convenient time to call. I'll keep it brief (under 10 minutes) to respect your time.

I'm most curious to hear your perspective on the most promising new solar technologies, which companies are developing them, and how you see solar competing over the next decade with other alternative energy options.

I appreciate your consideration.

Sincerely,

Jane Applicant
[phone number]

But don't simply depend on referrers.

Be fearless. Go to a company website and find their main number. Call and ask to be transferred to the department you're interested in. Tell whomever answers that you have a few questions about their area of expertise, and ask if you can schedule a brief (<10 minutes) time to chat with them at a time of their convenience. You'll be surprised how many folks are open to this. The worst they can say is 'no', at which point you thank them, hang up, and move on to the next website.

In my own career search, I was consistently amazed at how easy it was to locate and talk with just about anyone I wanted to. You just need to be tenacious. And polite. (Always, always be polite – there's no upside in not being so.)

Nailing the Informational interview
Okay, you've secured a call or an in-person meeting with a desirable contact. Now what?

You have two simple goals for these conversations:

1. Acquire information that will help advance your decision-making ability

2. Secure your next conversation

Goal #1 is dependent upon you being well prepared. Since your time is limited, write down the questions you most want answers to, in order of priority. Hopefully, your interviewee will get comfortable in the conversation and extend the time, if need be, to answer them all. But that might not happen, so get your most important questions addressed up front.

Also, don't be robotic about progressing through your questions. If the discussion veers into unplanned but useful territory, go with it.

Before the conversation, you also need to have assembled a list of your prepared asks (bring these up as your conversation is concluding).

At the top of this list, you should be asking for **referrals to other helpful people to talk with**, given the knowledge your interviewee now has about you. A good rule of thumb is to generate at least one new referral from every informational interview you have.

This 'daisy chain' of referrals is intended to keep you continuously zeroing in to the job territory that interests you most. If over time you begin to feel there's little more to learn from new referrals – and your interest the field is still high – it's a good sign that you're ready to commit to this career path.

Also consider asking your interviewee the following:

- *What **sources of information** do you find most valuable for staying well-informed?*
- *Given my goals and background, do you have any **advice** for me?*

Step 6: Identifying Target Industries, Roles & Co's

The former will help ensure that you're plugged in to the right intelligence. The latter is a dice roll – and you never know what unexpected insights might emerge.

Always follow up with a thank-you email. In my opinion, hand-written notes are no longer expected and often arrive too late to build momentum from the conversation. I would definitely send an email unless you get the sense that your interviewee is truly "old-school."

If you made any commitments during your conversation (sending along additional materials, etc.), be sure to follow through within 24 hours. Failing to do so sends a signal that you're not committed or not dependable, which will diminish their willingness to risk their reputation to help you.

Processing It All
If you are working hard at Step 6, you will be having 5 or more of these informational interviews a week. Combine that with all of the reading research and social media following that you're doing, and that's a tremendous amount of information to absorb.

Each week, you want to review the results from the prior week and ask yourself:

- *What new insights did I learn?*
- *Are those insights making the career path(s) I'm considering look more or less attractive?*
- *Which path(s) are looking better? Why?*
- *Which path(s) are looking worse? Why? Do I know enough now to strike any of these off of my consideration list?*
- *Which questions are the most important for me to answer next week?*
- *Which resources/people can I get these answers from?*

Navigating the 'Fallow' Period

Your coach will be the most useful resource in helping you articulate the answers to these questions and deciding what to do next.

Your support network of other job seekers will also be valuable in processing your conclusions. Explaining and defending your thinking will help you internally determine which decisions feel the most authentic to you.

Winnowing Down the Options: Completing Step 6
Remember, the goal for this Step is to end it with a much smaller number of potential career options than you started with.

The decision to drop options should get harder and harder as you proceed, indicating that you're increasing your progress towards territory that has true resonance for you.

But to move forward into Step 7 – pursing actual positions in your new field – winnow you must.

In the end, you want to have a relatively small number of options – say, 2 to 5 – that you have real trouble choosing among. These may be industries (e.g., agriculture), functional roles (e.g., product development), or a mixture of both.

Once you achieve this, be at peace. You've just identified your authentic work!

Now it's just a matter of persistence and time before you're actually living it. Both of those are within your control to influence. You're almost there.

For Inspiration: Dan's Story

I've recently gone through a pretty drastic career change. I spent the first 14 or so years since graduating from college bouncing around from one unfulfilling desk job to another. My major in college was financial management, and I worked many an analytical job at some prestigious finance/banking companies and a well-known and respected biotechnology firm. The money was good, as were the hours, but I hated the work. I hated being confined to a cubicle for 40-50 hours per week, and I hated how there seemed to be no direct correlation between the amount of work I did and my overall job satisfaction or compensation.

Soon after my wife and I were married, we moved across the country so that she could begin graduate school. Upon arriving in our new city, I found another job doing what I knew best and quickly grew tired of it. My wife's enrollment in graduate school was a huge catalyst for me – if she could allocate the time and resources towards career development and change, why couldn't I do the same thing?

Cooking had always been a huge passion of mine – I've always had a very healthy relationship with food – so enrolling in culinary school seemed like a logical choice. I came home one day and proclaimed to my skeptical wife that I wanted to open my own restaurant. That was the goal that sustained me through cooking school and motivated me to voraciously gobble my way through my curriculum. I very quickly took to my new studies and began immersing myself into the culinary world, taking on a variety of jobs and projects to further my growth in the field.

Navigating the 'Fallow' Period

I was very lucky in that this part of the transition was easy. After a little bit of convincing that I wasn't out of my mind, my wife became my biggest cheerleader. My manager at my cubicle-job work was also very supportive and allowed me to work part-time to help with the transition. We also had some money in savings so that eased our financial pressure a bit. And I had a plan – or so I thought.

After working in the field for a bit, I realized the restaurant path wasn't for me. About that time, my wife and I moved back home. That's when I really started to get nervous. The restaurant and food-service world at home was still foreign to me – all of my contacts and experience in this new industry were 3000 miles away. I felt very much like a fish out of water. In that sense, I realized how big of a leap-of-faith making these career-changing steps would require. I also learned the value of being patient and letting things run their course. I talked to many different folks representing all facets of the industry, and eventually, one random weekday afternoon, I found my calling.

After walking into a butcher shop, I knew I wanted to do something relating to meat. I was offered a job and spent the next year learning as much as I could, all the while continuing to refine my own vision. As my vision became clearer, again, I transitioned to a part-time role at the butcher shop. I spent the other part of my time honing my own recipes and beginning to lay the groundwork for what my business looks like today.

Now, I am happily self-employed, working as an artisan producer of high-quality deli meats. If you can put it between two slices of bread, I'll make it – pastrami, bacon, ham, sausage and much more. I sell meat directly to consumers and also run a successful catering business. I love working for myself. For the first time in my career, I feel happy and fulfilled.

Step 6: Identifying Target Industries, Roles & Co's

The high amount of dedication and perseverance I put into zeroing in on the "right" work for me definitely paid off. At the beginning, I didn't know how – or if – this process would work out. All I knew when I started was that I was unhappy and bitter and that I didn't want to keep living like that.

Looking back, I see these as the key ingredients: taking a leap of faith, support from a loved one, and a little bit of comfort in ambiguity because you won't have all the answers when you first get started.

STAGE THREE
Making a Successful Transition
Steps 7-9

Step 7: Pursing Work with Meaning in Your New Chosen Field

Finally(!) – it's time to focus on landing a specific job.

Review the short list of options you distilled in Step 6. Each of these should be extremely appealing to you, as well as in full harmony with the career values, goals, and requirements you laid out in STAGE ONE.

You should be able to clearly articulate the reasons why each option has made your list. If you can't, you haven't fully finished Step 6. (If this is the case, you should retrace and complete your work.)

But if you're ready, grab your list....

Painting Your Targets Clearly

As you've learned, the career search heavily draws on visualizing what success looks like.

So take your list of 'great-fit' options, and from it, create a new list of specific jobs you want at specific companies. These should be the jobs you think you would be happiest at – i.e., your "dream" jobs.

Given all that you know from your extensive research and informational conversations, envision what it would be like to have these jobs. *What excites you most about them? What your best understanding of what you'd do on a day-to-day basis? Why do you think the work will be rewarding?* Try to be as specific as possible in articulating your expectations.

Write down these expectations. You're going to return to them shortly.

Step 7: Pursuing Work With Meaning

Validating Your Assumptions

If you're going to throw yourself whole-heartedly into a new career, you want to make sure that your eyes are as wide open as possible when you decide to take that leap.

So, you'll want to get meaningful "hands-on" exposure before you decide to pursue a particular job.

There are a number of ways to do this:

- **Set up shadow days** - Follow someone who has the kind of job you're considering.
- **Do consulting projects** - Pick up consulting work in your target industry/ies.
- **Work for free** - Offer to work without pay on a part-time or time-bound basis for the company/ies that interest you most.
- **Get training** - Some career paths have on-board training programs that you can enroll in (e.g., First Responder and EMT training for those hoping to become Paramedics).

Do your best to pursue at least one of these approaches. The benefits far outweigh the investment:

- Doing so gives you a **'reality check' on your assumptions**.
    - *Does the actual work match your expectations?*
    - *Are the people you'll work with in this field a tribe you want to part of?*
- "Real-world" experience acts as a **catalyst for your candidacy**.
    - You now have relevant experience in the field you want to enter.
    - Taking on this work demonstrates commitment to the field.
    - It's much easier for employers to hire a 'known quantity'.

- ▪ If you've already been interning or consulting for a company, it's a lot easier for them to justify hiring you vs. another outside candidate they don't know as well.
- You can **leverage the relationships** you make during this period.
  - ○ Do well, and you'll suddenly have champions on the inside.
  - ○ The folks you work with will be excellent sources of internal information about potential positions, bosses, compensation, etc.
  - ○ They'll also be great information sources in the future if you enter this field. Always remember that people are more important than companies:
    - ▪ They may (and likely will) move on to other companies. Soon, you'll find there are people who know you at multiple companies that interest you.
  - ○ The immersive research you've done may actually make you more knowledgeable about the latest trends than those you're working with. They may come to value you as a source of insight as much as you do them.
- **Understand the pre-requisites** to get to the role you ultimately want.
  - ○ *What skills or experience are necessary? How long should it take to get those? Can you get those at lower levels within the company?*
  - ○ *Is there specific training, coursework, certification, or degrees you need? Are there positions at which you can initially enter the field before getting them?*

Take the findings from your time in the field and re-visit your shortlist. *Did your prior vision of the job hold up to the reality you experienced?*

Maybe you'll find you over-romanticized certain aspects that prove to be less interesting to you in practice. Or perhaps you'll get exposure to a different function that you end up preferring more than the one you initially were considering.

Whatever your learnings, adjust your shortlist accordingly.

Placing Your Bet
At this point, your shortlist should be no more than 1 to 3 options in length.

If longer than one, the options should be pretty similar – either related roles in the same industry (e.g., either Marketing or Sales for an organic food supplier), or the same role in related industries (e.g., Business Development in either the oil and gas or alternative fuels industries).

You are now at the stage where there's no more preparation left to be done.

Recognize that you've found your calling.

Actively make your decision that this path is the one you're going to dedicate the next chapter of your life to. Own that decision and the methodical process that has brought you to make it with certainty.

It's time to go for it.

Applying for (or Creating) Your New Position
Based on the work you have done so far in Steps 6 and 7, you should now know:

- What companies to target (and why)
- What role(s) you want there (and why)
- What qualifies you for these role(s)

- Where any weaknesses in your candidacy may lie (e.g., lack of experience)
- Industry insiders who may be able to help you

Through your researching, networking, and in-field work, you should have a pretty clear sense of the open positions at your target companies.

If so, it's always best if one of your inside contacts (or outside, if need be) can provide an endorsement on your behalf to the hiring manager. This will put you at the top of the consideration pile.

If you don't have a connection to the hiring manager, create one. At all costs, you DO NOT want to go in through the standard channel via Human Resources. Find a contact who can refer you to someone inside the company, whom you can then use for their influence to connect you with the hiring manager. Or find a way to contact the hiring manager directly (this is more risky, so exercise prudence).

Once in contact with the hiring manager, provide a succinct rationale for why you're applying, your understanding of the key needs of the job, why your qualifications are good match, and whom they can talk with to validate your points. (Emphasize skills, as well as relevant experience from the profession you're coming from.) Give them enough information to see that you thoroughly understand the need they're looking to fill, and that you have the passion and chops to fill it well.

Write this pitch down, and keep it to one page. You'll likely need to email it as a cover letter. But you may also need to provide it verbally in an interview, so practice until it flows naturally, concisely, and convincingly.

DO NOT send your resume until requested to do so. If you've connected well with the hiring manager, receiving your resume will simply be a formality. For reasons already discussed, don't lead with it.

Also, even though you will be chomping at the bit to get hired and started in your new career, keep your enthusiasm in check. DO NOT let your hunger for the position compel you to come on too strong. Hiring managers work at their own pace, often slower than even they want – which may well be why they're hiring. So don't hound them or allow them to perceive that you're trying to rush their decision-making. It can make you look too high-maintenance to work with (or maybe even a little psycho).

Handle the ensuing interviews, etc., with class, and, while being careful not to go overboard, let your genuine passion for the role shine through.

You may not get the first few positions you apply for. But if you stay positive and persevere – and integrate any constructive feedback you receive from interviewers along the way – your odds of receiving the news you want are extremely high.

Remember, in cracking into your new chosen field, it doesn't matter how many times you hear "no." Because you only need to hear "yes" once.

Fostering Serendipity
And now to let you in on a little secret: No matter how diligently you apply the instructions detailed in this guide, luck will play a huge role in landing your 'best fit' job.

But this won't be random luck. It will be luck you create.

Making a Successful Transition

As you make connections in the industry, attend events, visit companies, and so forth, you are creating tendrils of opportunity. These extend out like ripples on the water. Most subside unnoticed, but the more involved you become, the higher the odds are that your passion and your "fit" will catch someone's attention.

This means that after a while, in addition to your focused pursuit of opportunity, *opportunity starts finding you.*

Be aware of this potential, and open yourself to it. In more cases than you might expect, fulfilled workers found their jobs in a way they didn't initially expect.

The same is true for me, as well as for my business partner, Chris. Serendipity – and our openness to it – played a huge role in how we ended up where we are.

So, as you pursue the opportunities you've laid out for yourself, keep yourself flexible enough to react to good fortune if and when it presents itself.

You don't need serendipity to land your job. And there's no guarantee you'll experience it, so you shouldn't count on it. But given all of your planning and hard work, the odds for it aren't bad.

Completing Step 7
By the end of Step 7, you should have a number of irons in the fire with *actual* companies regarding *actual* jobs that you *actually* want.

One (and likely more) is eventually going to result in an offer. Hooray!

Step 8 will help ensure that whatever offer you accept is best suited to your requirements.

Step 8: Landing the Right Opportunity for You

At some point all of your hard work will pay off. A company you want will offer you a job you want.

First things first: Break out the champagne! You have successfully transitioned from a 'bad fit' career to a 'great-fit' one. That's absolutely tremendous.

But be smart in the midst of your joy. The decisions you make now will have long-lasting repercussions.

Some advice to consider when evaluating your offer:

Limit Compromises
Within reason, stick to your guns to get the work you want, the way you want it. If you're given an offer lacking essential elements (for instance, a great role with a bad boss), it's actually better to pass.

I realize that may sound crazy. But it often takes years to work past the constraints of your initial position. Instead of leaping at a deficient offer, you need to look at it as validation that you are indeed a 'great-fit' candidate, and that another – better – opportunity is coming.

In a lot of cases, the offer will be adjusted to better meet your requirements, as the company values you and doesn't want to have go back to the drawing board. And if the company doesn't show any accommodation to your requests, that's a pretty clear sign that you'll be better served taking more time to find the right fit.

Stay Grounded
The above said, also take care not to sabotage your success. Remember that humble beginnings in the right field are vastly preferable to a higher status role in another.

Making a Successful Transition

Your initial impulse may be to grab for as much of your "wish list" as possible when an offer arrives, fearing that the chance may not come again. Fight that.

Instead, keep the big-picture goal in mind. As experienced coaches advise, *your best exit may be behind you.* By that, they mean that the right work matters more at this point than title or compensation level.

If you finally have an offer to do the work that you truly think is best suited for you, that's an incredible gift. Take it. If indeed you've found your calling, you will excel. And because of that, you'll soon advance to the level you deserve.

Keep Your Focus
Stay mindful of the fact that you will need to continue to earn your new career going forward.

As a new entrant in your field, there is still much you don't know. You are not a seasoned expert yet.

To help you on your way, create SMART (Specific, Measurable, Attainable, Relevant, Timely) goals early in your new career for your performance and development for the first 6 and 12 months. Make sure your manager and/or work peers and partners are aware of these goals, in agreement with them, and willing to support you in achieving them. Arrange review of progress to these goals with your boss every 3 months (at a minimum).

By being clear up front with everyone about your needs and expectations, your odds of meeting them will skyrocket.

Completing Step 8

The goal of Step 8 is to see you safely to the completion of your transition.

Don't let the excitement of receiving your first offer result in poor decision-making at the last mile.

Be smart and resolute. You've earned the offer you want.

Step 9: Beginning Your Authentic Career

As you step into the daily joy of practicing your "authentic" work, also take time to both look back and look ahead.

Look Back
Thank everyone who played a constructive role in your transition. Your coach, advisors, emotional supporters, networkers, informational interviewees – anyone who contributed to your happy ending.

For those who made the biggest impact, risk being overly generous in showing your gratitude. Any gift you offer will pale in comparison to the value they've helped you to unlock in your life.

Many of these folks were emotionally invested in your success and will be thrilled to hear of your good news. And many will valuable contacts for you in your new field, so you'll want to keep those relationships well tended.

Look at the other aspects of your life that may have been crowded out during the intensity of your career search. Did friendships, your fitness level, or your hobbies atrophy due to lack of attention? If so, start making a concerted effort to re-invest. A healthy life balance will position you well for early success in your new work.

Look Forward
Assuming you've already set down your 6- and 12-month career goals from Step 8, ask yourself:

- *Who can serve as my advisors going forward?*
  - Your former advisors may or may not be suitable for the new career path you've chosen.
- *Can I find a mentor?*

- Recruit someone with decades of experience in the work you are doing or plan to do.
- *How do I want my career to evolve from here?*
  - Work with your mentor, advisors, and/or career coach in developing a detailed vision for the next 5, 10, 20 years of your career.
- *How can I give back?*
  - You've been extremely fortunate to make your transition. Be giving of your time and expertise to others considering taking the same leap. Give informational interviews. Use your network for the benefit of others. Serve as an advisor. Be a mentor.

Prepare for Prosperity

Given your excellent fit for the work you're now engaged in, you will likely outperform relative to others in your field. You will begin to amass capital – both financial and social – as a result.

Prepare in advance for what you plan to do with these profits. If you feel you don't have the know-how to manage them wisely and prudently, find qualified advisers to help.

Realize the Journey is the Destination

As you grow in your new career, you'll quickly realize that fulfillment comes from continual growth. Don't rest on your laurels.

Of course, there is the chance your first job in your new field doesn't turn out to be the 'great fit' that you thought it would be. If it's not, what should you do?

Start by articulating which of your requirements it's not fully meeting. Discuss these with your managers and/or partners. Can these shortcomings be addressed?

If not, create capacity to revisit Steps 7 and 8. While it may sound discouraging to have to re-engage back into the career search, the odds for success are now even more in your favor. You now have deeper, more relevant work experience in the field, and a better understanding of the job requirements that are most important to you.

You'll likely find that it takes a lot less time and effort to land the next, better, offer.

Be at Peace
Your long journey through transition is over.

Relax. Take some time off to recharge and enjoy the absence of anxiety.

Be proud of yourself. Feel excited about the future.

Be at peace.

Completing Step 9
Well, you've done it.

You've made your way to your authentic career.

That's something very few people can claim. And you worked hard – very hard – to achieve this.

At this point, there's nothing more for me to add except to say how happy I am for you. I wish you the best of success from here.

And I have one ask. When you feel comfortably settled in your new career, please visit the Finding Your Authentic Career Group at PeakProsperity.com and share your story.

Simply write a few sentences (or paragraphs) about your goals, your fears, your journey, your final results, and any key lessons you learned along the way.

Models of success offer insight and inspiration to those considering following in the footsteps of your courage.

With your voice, we can help others end up as happy as you.

All the best,
Adam

For Inspiration: Adam's Story

Late 2009: *Stress and anxiety defined my world. But on the surface, no one suspected that.*

I was a Vice President at the Fortune 300 Silicon Valley tech giant I worked at, about to celebrate my 9th anniversary there. I had arrived there after a successful start-up stint, and before that, an MBA from Stanford and a few years at a Wall Street bulge bracket firm.

My career appeared to be progressing right on schedule. So what was there to worry about?

As my business partner, Chris Martenson, likes to point out: When what we think is out of alignment with what we do, anxiety thrives.

And that's where I was: on a career trajectory that I believed to be woefully not relevant to the future I saw coming.

Outside of the office, I had spent years learning about the numerous unsustainable macro trends warned about in The Crash Course and related materials. The bursting of the tech bubble, the larger housing bubble, and then the Great Contraction of 2008 added clear validity (in my eyes) to these warnings.

I felt a strong compulsion to position my family -- and others if possible -- prudently in advance of the full force of these macro trends arriving.

Yet there I was, toiling away in Silicon Valley suburbia on initiatives that took none of these concerns into account. The work demanded long hours, at a desk under artificial lighting, with people whose faith in technology to overcome all problems felt naively dogmatic. I felt trapped and extremely vulnerable.

Both my emotional and physical health, as well as the relationships I valued, were paying an increasing price as these pressures built. But I had a tremendously hard time giving up on the status quo, because the uncertainty of taking a new path – especially when I had no idea what that path would be – seemed too great a risk for my 'provider' instinct to tolerate.

Finally, the fear of continued inaction eclipsed my fear of uncertainty. I took the very bold (for me) step of giving notice at work without a clue what I'd do next.

For such a big risk, I knew I needed to stack the odds for success as much in my favor as possible; so I began recruiting experts to assist me. And as I put their advice into practice, I began a learning process that culminated in the valuable holistic understanding of the career search process this book captures.

It's now 2012. *I'm approaching the 3-year anniversary of the best job I've ever had (by a long shot) as the co-founder of PeakProsperity.com*

My days are filled with purpose. The work I do is the work I want to do. I feel like my energies and abilities are being put to their best use. And, from the feedback we receive from our customers, it seems like we're having good success in our mission to help people improve their quality of life.

And funnily enough, while there's a lot more business risk in this entrepreneurial venture compared to my previous corporate roles, I sleep much better at night. That's because my actions are now much more aligned with my priorities.

Making a Successful Transition

My wife and I moved my family to a rural community, with deep agricultural roots, and a community that prizes resilience and local resources. We both have careers we're fully passionate about, and are our own employers – so there's no worry of waking up in the morning to learn of surprise layoffs. We have much more time to spend with our children and get involved in the community. We finally feel we're living the life we were meant to live.

If there's one thing I'd highlight for someone reading this who, like I was, is yearning to change their professional destiny, it's this: **Success is possible. Probable, even.** *It just takes a commitment to see the work through.*

Your authentic work is out there waiting. Now go find it.

Happy hunting!

ENDNOTES: WEB LINKS

Introduction
- www.peakprosperity.com
- www.peakprosperity.com/crashcourse
- www.peakprosperity.com/blog/82100/my-career-transition-story

Step 1
- http://en.wikipedia.org/wiki/Know_thyself
- http://finance.yahoo.com/blogs/daily-ticker/most-americans-not-happy-yahoo-finance-parade-survey-112833013.html
- http://www.myersbriggs.org/my-mbti-personality-type/mbti-basics/
- http://www.myersbriggs.org/frequently-asked-questions/ways-to-take-the-mbti/
- https://www.mbticomplete.com/contents/learnmore.aspx
- https://www.gallupstrengthscenter.com/Purchase
- http://www.strengthsfinder.com/home.aspx
- http://www.careerleader.com/individuals.html
- http://www.jocrf.org
- www.peakprosperity.com/page/what-should-i-do
- http://fiveoclockclub.com
- http://fiveoclockclub.com/for-individuals/book-a-private-coach
- http://fiveoclockclub.com
- http://www.careerleader.com/career.html
- http://www.yelp.com

Step 5
- www.craigslist.org
- www.peakprosperity.com/groups
- http://groups.yahoo.com
- www.ning.com

- www.linkedin.com
- www.facebook.com
- www.twitter.com
- www.meetup.com/find

Step 8
- http://en.wikipedia.org/wiki/SMART_criteria

Step 9
- http://www.peakprosperity.com/endorsed-financial-advisors
- http://www.peakprosperity.com/group/finding-your-authentic-career
- www.peakprosperity.com/crashcourse

3161030R00056

Made in the USA
San Bernardino, CA
11 July 2013